5 Minutes to Happiness

Start living the life you want now...

We create our books with love and great care.

Yet mistakes can always happen. For any issues with your journal, such as faulty binding, printing errors, or something else, please do not hesitate to contact us at: **hello@happinesscreators.com**.
We will make sure you get a replacement copy immediately.

For any suggestions or questions regarding our books, please contact us at: **hello@happinesscreators.com**

ISBN: 978-8412487428

Without your voice we don't exist.
Please, support us and leave a review!

Thank you!

Happiness Through the Power of Gratitude

Do you want to be happy? Be grateful.

Practicing gratitude is one of the simplest and most effective things you can do to transform your life. Numerous studies have shown that people who regularly take time to notice things they are grateful for enjoy better sleep, better relationships, greater resolve towards achieving their goals, show more compassion and kindness, and, most importantly, are overall happier.

Gratitude doesn't have to be only about the big things. It's in the simple pleasures too: you can be thankful for a nice cup of coffee, a sunny winter day, or that adorable silly butt-wiggle dance your dog makes when you come home.

As long as you practice it regularly by keeping a gratitude journal and writing brief reflections on the moments you are thankful for you can easily enhance your overall well-being and contentment in life.

What about you? What are you grateful for today?

BEFORE YOU START:

There will be days when life feels overwhelming, when every moment seems to challenge your peace. There might be times of grief, anger, or betrayal that make expressing gratitude seem almost impossible. When such days come, and they will, remember to revisit the following 3 pages. They'll be here, ready to shine a light during your darkest moments.

A Thoughtful Reflection for Challenging Times

LIST THINGS YOU HAVE EVERY DAY and you can be grateful for but you rarely or never manage to appreciate.

Just a hint: electricity, running cold and hot water, eyesight, hands, legs, etc.

LIST PEOPLE YOU ARE GRATEFUL FOR; not only people that you have in your life, but also people that you have never met but have managed to inspire you or teach you something by their story or actions.

Just a hint: your mother, best friend, high school teacher, Frida Kahlo, Oprah, etc.

LIST NEGATIVE EVENTS THAT LED TO POSITIVE CHANGES IN YOUR LIFE.

Just a hint: hard breakup only to begin a better relationship, loss of a job only to find something else that you love doing, broken screen of your phone only to buy a new one with a better camera, etc.

LIST MOMENTS IN YOUR LIFE WHEN YOU FELT PROUD OF YOURSELF.

Just a hint: when you didn't give up even though it got tough, that time you made your daughter smile, that time you picked up someone else's litter, etc.

LIST THE TOP THINGS THAT MAKE YOU FEEL BETTER.

Just a hint: a favorite song, a night out with a friend, watching episodes of a favorite TV show, dancing alone when no one is watching, etc.

LIST THE MOST IMPORTANT EVENTS IN YOUR LIFE THAT YOU ARE GRATEFUL FOR.

You deserve to be

STOP.

Long-term consistency trumps short-term intensity.

This powerful principle can be applied to any aspect in life, whether trying to lose weight, start a career, or maintain a romantic relationship.

Or to put it in straightforward examples:

- *Simple everyday kind words and actions are better than grand one-time romantic gestures.*
- *A little yoga often is better than a lot but done rarely.*
- *Dedicating five minutes daily to a gratitude journal is more effective than writing for hours on end, but only sporadically.*

THINK.

GO ON.

DATE Mo Tu We Th Fr Sa Su ___/___/___

I am grateful for...

List 3 small things that brought you joy today.

DATE Mo Tu We Th Fr Sa Su ___/___/___

I am grateful for...

Give yourself 3 genuine compliments.

DATE Mo Tu We Th Fr Sa Su ___/___/___

I am grateful for...

What are you looking forward to tomorrow or in the upcoming week?

DATE Mo Tu We Th Fr Sa Su ___/___/___

I am grateful for...

Who are the people whose company you enjoyed today?

STOP.

You can't win in life
if you are losing in mind.
Change your thoughts
and it will change your life.

THINK.

GO ON.

DATE Mo Tu We Th Fr Sa Su ___/___/___

I am grateful for...

Name 3 beautiful things that you saw today.

Mo Tu We Th Fr Sa Su

DATE ___/___/___

I am grateful for...

What happy memory makes you smile every time you think about it?

STOP.

Every day may not be good
but there is something good
in every day.

REMEMBER.

GO ON.

Mo Tu We Th Fr Sa Su

DATE ___/___/___

I am grateful for...

What is one kind thing you did for someone else recently?

THIS WEEK'S REFLECTION

What are your superpowers?

Most of us easily identify our weaknesses, but struggle to name our natural strengths and talents. Not only that, but when we think of improving ourselves, we normally think of a weakness that we have, not a strength.

But research shows that people who recognize and use their strengths are generally more successful. We experience faster growth if we focus on developing our strengths rather than trying to eliminate our weaknesses.

If at this point you think, "I am not really excelling at anything", stop! Everybody has their own strengths. Work on developing them and turn them into your superpowers.

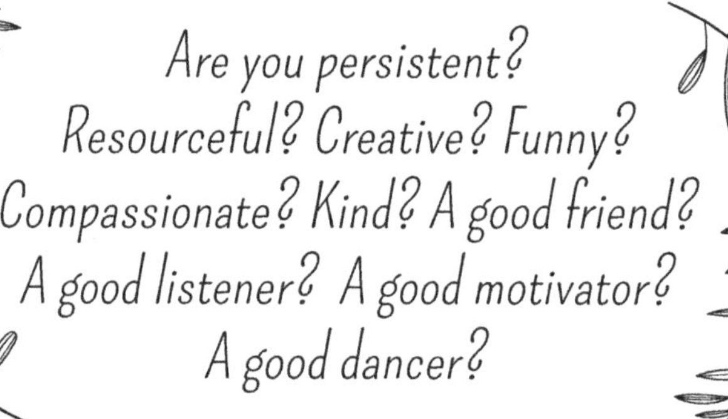

Finish the sentence: I am...

Think of 3 good things that happened this week:

Mo Tu We Th Fr Sa Su

DATE ___/___/___

I am grateful for...

List 3 things (or more) that you like about yourself.

Mo Tu We Th Fr Sa Su

DATE ___/___/___

I am grateful for...

What's one thing you did well today?

Mo Tu We Th Fr Sa Su

DATE ___/___/___

I am grateful for...

Write about the last compliment you received and how it made you feel.

DATE Mo Tu We Th Fr Sa Su ___/___/___

I am grateful for...

What are the things you want to remember from today?

STOP.

When life gives you lemons say 'thank you' and keep them because, hey, free lemons!

SMILE.

GO ON.

DATE Mo Tu We Th Fr Sa Su ___/___/___

I am grateful for...

What self-care activities bring you feelings of joy and calm?

DATE Mo Tu We Th Fr Sa Su ___/___/___

I am grateful for...

Who is your favorite person in the world?

STOP.

Happiness is not a big thing.
It is a million
little things.

REMEMBER.
GO ON.

DATE Mo Tu We Th Fr Sa Su ___/___/___

I am grateful for...

Make some time to listen to your favorite songs today. What are they?

THIS WEEK'S REFLECTION

Try this smile challenge:

Smile at yourself in the mirror

first thing in the morning for at least a week.

It might feel silly at first but smiling has many benefits for your well-being. Smiling slows the heart and relaxes the body, releases endorphins and diminishes stress hormones, increases productivity, and strengthens the immune system.

Smiling, as it turns out, prompts your brain to produce feel-good hormones and activates your brain's happiness circuitry. As a result, smiling makes you feel good regardless of your current mood in the moment.
So go ahead and

Think of your favorite moments from this week that put a smile on your face:

Think of 3 good things that happened this week:

Mo Tu We Th Fr Sa Su

DATE ___/___/___

I am grateful for...

Write a positive affirmation that resonates with you today.

Mo Tu We Th Fr Sa Su

DATE ___/___/___

I am grateful for...

What is an element of your daily routine that brings you comfort?

Mo Tu We Th Fr Sa Su

DATE ___/___/___

I am grateful for...

What is one movie or tv show that always makes you happy?

DATE Mo Tu We Th Fr Sa Su ___/___/___

I am grateful for...

Write one word that describes your mood right now and why.

STOP.

Hakuna Matata.

SMILE.

GO ON.

DATE Mo Tu We Th Fr Sa Su ___/___/___

I am grateful for...

Let yourself dream a little. Close your eyes and

imagine your best possible self.

Imagine the person you want to become, how you will feel, think and behave, how others will know you are at your best.

Mo Tu We Th Fr Sa Su

DATE ___/___/___

I am grateful for...

☼

Name something you love about your body that isn't related to what it looks like.

☽

STOP.

Feelings are much like waves.
We can't stop them from coming
but we can choose which one to surf.

THINK.

GO ON.

Mo Tu We Th Fr Sa Su

DATE ___/___/___

I am grateful for...

☼

List one thing you're looking forward to.

☽

THIS WEEK'S REFLECTION

Do you ever say thank you to yourself?

If you are thinking "I didn't do enough" or "I didn't exercise" or "I didn't eat healthy" or "I keep making the same mistakes", it may be a sign that you don't appreciate yourself enough.

Thank yourself for the efforts. Thank yourself for trying to be better, to learn and grow. Or thank yourself for the awareness of what you need to change.

If you make a conscious effort to appreciate all the things you do, no matter how small, you will learn to truly love and appreciate yourself.

Think of 3 good things that happened this week:

DATE Mo Tu We Th Fr Sa Su ___/___/___

I am grateful for...

What made you laugh today?

DATE Mo Tu We Th Fr Sa Su ___/___/___

I am grateful for...

What's a recent victory, big or small?

DATE Mo Tu We Th Fr Sa Su ___/___/___

I am grateful for...

What's something that will make tomorrow easier or more comfortable for you?

Mo Tu We Th Fr Sa Su

DATE ___/___/___

I am grateful for...

List the people you loved talking to today.

STOP.

Appreciate life as it happens.
Moments will soon pass
and you will wish
you had treasured them more.

THINK.
GO ON.

Mo Tu We Th Fr Sa Su

DATE ___/___/___

I am grateful for...

What's a simple pleasure you're grateful for?

A SPECIAL MESSAGE FROM OUR TEAM:

Thank you!
We appreciate you!
We'll keep working hard to deliver quality books and journals to make your life better.

Are you enjoying this journal so far?

We'd be incredibly grateful if you could share your experience. With fewer than 1% of readers leaving reviews, your thoughts are more important than ever.

Please, take just a moment of your time to leave a review. It makes a big difference and helps us immensely.

In return we promise you that we will continuously improve in every single way and work hard to provide you with the best journaling experience possible.

Fill this jar with affirmations:

THANK YOU FOR YOUR TRUST!

GO ON.

DATE Mo Tu We Th Fr Sa Su ___/___/___

I am grateful for...

Name someone who helped you recently.

STOP.

Don't give up on your dreams!
Keep sleeping.

SMILE.
GO ON.

DATE Mo Tu We Th Fr Sa Su ___/___/___

I am grateful for...

Reflect on a book, movie, or show that you are thankful for and the impact it had on you.

THIS WEEK'S REFLECTION

The Power of Positive Thinking

Noticing the good things in your life is a skill that can be improved and developed. Even if you are not a naturally optimistic person, daily practice can make it easier over time.

At the end of each day consciously try to rewind in your mind the events of that day and look for one little good thing. And then another one. And another one.

The more you focus on the positives, the more you'll notice them in your life. Like your favorite song playing randomly on the radio. Or the smell outside after the rain has stopped. Or climbing into bed when you have fresh sheets. Or a compliment from a colleague that you normally wouldn't notice or even believe.

Think of 3 good things that happened this week:

Next week try to

go to bed always with a positive thought.

Focus on one positive thing that happened during the day or one positive thing of tomorrow you are excited about.

DATE Mo Tu We Th Fr Sa Su ___/___/___

I am grateful for...

What went great today?

DATE Mo Tu We Th Fr Sa Su ___/___/___

I am grateful for...

What's something you're glad you have in your home?

DATE Mo Tu We Th Fr Sa Su ___/___/___

I am grateful for...

What food did you enjoy today?

Mo Tu We Th Fr Sa Su

DATE ___/___/____

I am grateful for...

Which song made you feel good recently?

STOP.

When things get tough remember: better days are coming. They are called Saturday and Sunday.

SMILE.

GO ON.

Mo Tu We Th Fr Sa Su

DATE ___/___/____

I am grateful for...

What made you smile today?

DATE Mo Tu We Th Fr Sa Su ___/___/___

I am grateful for...

Write the name of a person you're happy to know.

STOP.

You are just blessed to be here – fact.

REMEMBER.

GO ON.

DATE Mo Tu We Th Fr Sa Su ___/___/___

I am grateful for...

Write down one thing you're looking forward to learning.

Write yourself a love letter.

That's right. A love letter.
This is one of the most effective methods to practice self-love and a great tool that can calm and center you in times of crisis when everything seems upside down. You can read it anytime you need a little nudge to get up and move on.

How to write your love letter?

» Don't type. There are proven psychological benefits to writing things down by hand.

» Start with a salutation that will make you smile.

» Include affirmative sentences about your character, body, goals, achievements, values, etc.

» And finally, don't be shy or modest and forget about your insecurities. Everyone is worthy of love. You don't need anyone's approval (even yours) to deserve that love.

Think of 3 good things that happened this week:

Mo Tu We Th Fr Sa Su

DATE ___/___/___

I am grateful for...

Write down today's best moment.

Mo Tu We Th Fr Sa Su

DATE ___/___/___

I am grateful for...

Name a smell or scent you enjoyed today.

Mo Tu We Th Fr Sa Su

DATE ___/___/___

I am grateful for...

What's one comfort you enjoyed today?

DATE Mo Tu We Th Fr Sa Su ___/___/___

I am grateful for...

Recall a childhood memory that still makes you giggle.

STOP.

Just in case no one told you today:
Good morning!
You are doing great.
I believe in you.
Nice butt.

SMILE.
GO ON.

DATE Mo Tu We Th Fr Sa Su ___/___/___

I am grateful for...

Write a joke that made you laugh.

Mo Tu We Th Fr Sa Su

DATE ___/___/___

I am grateful for...

What piece of technology made your day easier?

STOP.

When life gets tough remember: so are you!

REMEMBER.

GO ON.

Mo Tu We Th Fr Sa Su

DATE ___/___/___

I am grateful for...

Write the name of a song that uplifted you.

Know who you are.

Take time to know what you like, what you don't, your needs, your values, your standards, your goals, your strengths and weaknesses, what you cannot tolerate and what the essentials in your life are.

Only then you can learn to accept who you are and live your life authentically.

Describe yourself using
the first 5 words that come to your mind.

List 5 words that you'd like to use to describe yourself.

Think of 3 good things that happened this week:

DATE Mo Tu We Th Fr Sa Su ___/___/___

I am grateful for...

Write about a hobby that makes you lose track of time.

DATE Mo Tu We Th Fr Sa Su ___/___/___

I am grateful for...

Name the best drink you had today.

DATE Mo Tu We Th Fr Sa Su ___/___/___

I am grateful for...

Name a convenience you're thankful for.

DATE Mo Tu We Th Fr Sa Su ___/___/___

I am grateful for...

What's a recent purchase you're thankful for?

STOP.

The antidote to fear is gratitude.
The antidote to anger is gratitude.
You can't feel fear or anger while
feeling gratitude at the same time.

THINK.
GO ON.

DATE Mo Tu We Th Fr Sa Su ___/___/___

I am grateful for...

Write about a funny "fail" you had that turned into a good story.

DATE Mo Tu We Th Fr Sa Su ___/___/___

I am grateful for...

What gives you hope for a bright future?

STOP.

Choose to be optimistic. It feels better.

THINK.
GO ON.

DATE Mo Tu We Th Fr Sa Su ___/___/___

I am grateful for...

Name a person in your life who has made a positive impact and write about why you're grateful for them.

THIS WEEK'S REFLECTION

Trade your expectations for appreciation.

Expectation is about waiting for something or looking back on what you did or didn't get, and focusing on what you lack at the moment.

If you are waiting for a future event or an external change to bring you happiness, you might never truly be happy. Instead, seek happiness within by appreciating what you currently have and what surrounds you at this moment. Focusing on the present like this is a far more fulfilling way to live.

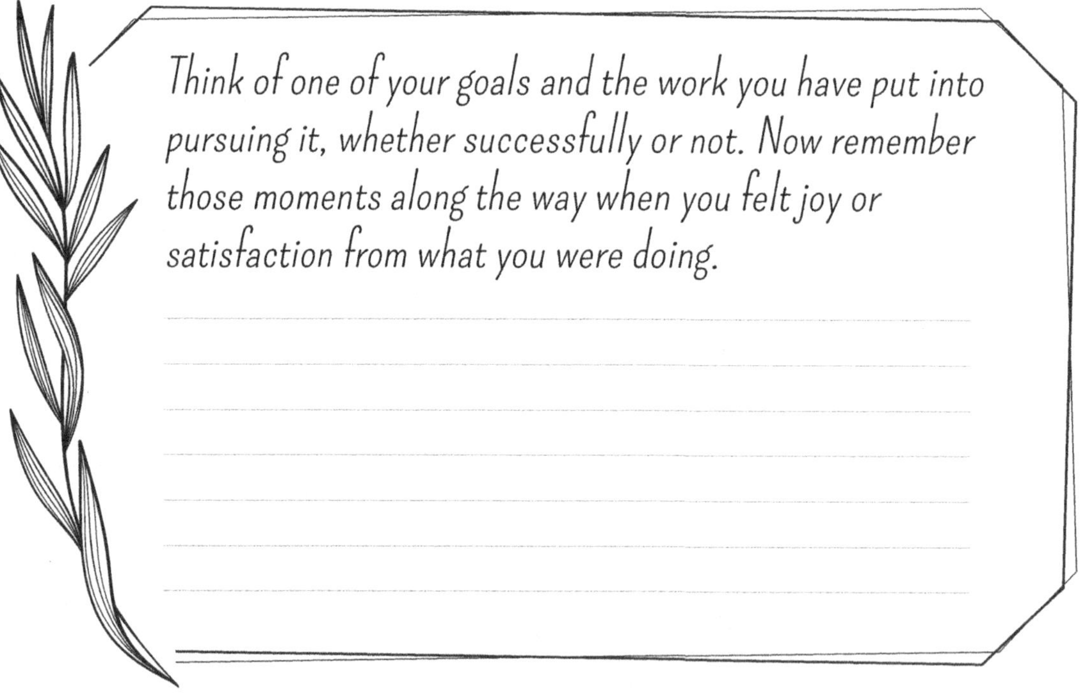

Think of one of your goals and the work you have put into pursuing it, whether successfully or not. Now remember those moments along the way when you felt joy or satisfaction from what you were doing.

Think of 3 good things that happened this week:

Mo Tu We Th Fr Sa Su

DATE ___/___/___ *I am grateful for...*

Think of when you appreciated someone's effort, regardless of the outcome.

Mo Tu We Th Fr Sa Su

DATE ___/___/___ *I am grateful for...*

What's something that worked well for you today?

Mo Tu We Th Fr Sa Su

DATE ___/___/___ *I am grateful for...*

Write down the best thing you tasted today.

DATE Mo Tu We Th Fr Sa Su ___/___/___

I am grateful for...

Write about a simple daily convenience you often take for granted.

STOP.

Stop focusing on how stressed you are and remember how blessed you are.

THINK.

GO ON.

DATE Mo Tu We Th Fr Sa Su ___/___/___

I am grateful for...

Name three small things you appreciated today that you hadn't planned or expected.

DATE Mo Tu We Th Fr Sa Su ___/___/___

I am grateful for...

Name a favorite comfort food you enjoyed recently.

STOP.

Breathe. Don't let a bad day make you feel like you have a bad life.

THINK.

GO ON.

DATE Mo Tu We Th Fr Sa Su ___/___/___

I am grateful for...

Consider a part of your day that was better than you expected. What made it that way?

THIS WEEK'S REFLECTION

A Simple Hug as a Natural Anti-Depressant

Scientists found that during 20 seconds of continuous hugging we release oxytocin, a hormone that relaxes us and lowers anxiety.

Just the simple act of touch also seems to boost oxytocin release. Giving someone a massage, cuddling, making love, or giving someone a hug leads to higher levels of this hormone and a greater sense of well-being.

Who are the people that mean the most to you?
Give them a hug and tell them you love them.

Think of 3 good things that happened this week:

Mo Tu We Th Fr Sa Su

DATE ____/____/____

I am grateful for...

What is something that works well in your life right now?

Mo Tu We Th Fr Sa Su

DATE ____/____/____

I am grateful for...

Who made you smile or laugh today, and why?

Mo Tu We Th Fr Sa Su

DATE ____/____/____

I am grateful for...

Who would you thank today for their support or companionship?

Mo Tu We Th Fr Sa Su

DATE ___/___/___

I am grateful for...

Describe an awkward moment that you can now laugh about.

STOP.

Strength does not come from winning. Your struggles develop your strengths. When you go through great hardships and decide not to surrender, that is a strength.

THINK.

GO ON.

Mo Tu We Th Fr Sa Su

DATE ___/___/___

I am grateful for...

What's one thing you accomplished today, no matter how small?

DATE Mo Tu We Th Fr Sa Su ___/___/___

I am grateful for...

☼

Think of a time when you tried something new and it didn't go as planned, in a funny way.

☽

STOP.

You can.
End of story.

REMEMBER.
GO ON.

DATE Mo Tu We Th Fr Sa Su ___/___/___

I am grateful for...

☼

Think about a time when someone appreciated your work, and how it made you feel.

☽

Music heals the soul.

Music is recognized as an evidence-based form of therapy; it can lower your blood pressure, help you manage pain, help alleviate the symptoms of depression, anxiety, and other mood disorders, and increase motivation.

If you had to name a song for your current life, which one would it be?

Why?

If you could change things around, what would you want your main song to be?

Think of 3 good things that happened this week:

DATE Mo Tu We Th Fr Sa Su ___/___/___

I am grateful for...

What songs cheer you up or relax you on a tough day?

DATE Mo Tu We Th Fr Sa Su ___/___/___

I am grateful for...

What's something beautiful in your home?

DATE Mo Tu We Th Fr Sa Su ___/___/___

I am grateful for...

Write down the best thing you experienced this morning.

Mo Tu We Th Fr Sa Su

DATE ___/___/___

I am grateful for...

☼

Who is someone that always listens when you need to talk?

☽

STOP.

The best things in life aren't things.

THINK.

GO ON.

Mo Tu We Th Fr Sa Su

DATE ___/___/___

I am grateful for...

☼

Write about how expressing appreciation has impacted your mental well-being.

☽

Mo Tu We Th Fr Sa Su

DATE ___/___/___ I am grateful for...

Write down one thing that relaxed you.

STOP.

Nothing is impossible.
The word itself says "I'm possible".

REMEMBER.
GO ON.

Mo Tu We Th Fr Sa Su

DATE ___/___/___ I am grateful for...

Close your eyes. Identify and list every sound that you hear over the span of 2 minutes.

THIS WEEK'S REFLECTION

Schedule the time for what makes you happy.

You probably won't enjoy taking time for yourself if you know there is something else you need to be doing. So, schedule the time for the little things that make you feel good. Watch an episode of your favorite TV show, listen to your favorite music, take a bath, etc.

Doing more of what makes you happy is not a luxury, it is essential for your well-being.

Think of 3 good things that happened this week:

Mo Tu We Th Fr Sa Su

DATE ___/___/___

I am grateful for...

Recall a time when you and a friend couldn't stop laughing.

Mo Tu We Th Fr Sa Su

DATE ___/___/___

I am grateful for...

Is there an upcoming event you are looking forward to?

Mo Tu We Th Fr Sa Su

DATE ___/___/___

I am grateful for...

Write about a moment of peace or stillness you experienced today.

Mo Tu We Th Fr Sa Su

DATE ___/___/___

I am grateful for...

What's the most humorous gift you've ever received?

STOP.

Smile.

There is chocolate, wine and coffee for every occasion.

SMILE.

GO ON.

Mo Tu We Th Fr Sa Su

DATE ___/___/___

I am grateful for...

Name a funny autocorrect fail from a text message this week.

Mo Tu We Th Fr Sa Su

DATE ___/___/___

I am grateful for...

What's something you've learned recently that you're grateful for?

STOP.

You've been criticizing yourself for years and it hasn't worked. Try approving of yourself and see what happens.

THINK.

GO ON.

Mo Tu We Th Fr Sa Su

DATE ___/___/___

I am grateful for...

Write something positive about yourself.

THIS WEEK'S REFLECTION

It is hard to stay strong, happy and hopeful, and love yourself 100% of the time, when hard times hit. It is easy to get lost in the negative self-talk spiral when you feel down.

Don't beat yourself up for your negative feelings and emotions. They are something you experience; they don't define you. Remember,

You walk in the rain,
and you feel the rain,
but, importantly,
you are not the rain.

Focus on what you can do to feel better.
Create a plan for coping with your negative emotions and list 5 very easy small things you can do to brighten your day.

Think of 3 good things that happened this week:

Mo Tu We Th Fr Sa Su

DATE ___/___/___

I am grateful for...

What is your emotional state at this moment? Name it without judgment.

Mo Tu We Th Fr Sa Su

DATE ___/___/___

I am grateful for...

What were you doing the last time you lost track of time?

Mo Tu We Th Fr Sa Su

DATE ___/___/___

I am grateful for...

Write down one thing about yourself you've come to accept and appreciate.

DATE Mo Tu We Th Fr Sa Su ___/___/___

I am grateful for...

Who would you like to thank and/or acknowledge today?

STOP.

Feeling gratitude
and not expressing it
is like wrapping a present
and not giving it.

THINK.
GO ON.

DATE Mo Tu We Th Fr Sa Su ___/___/___

I am grateful for...

Today thank yourself for the mistakes, because you learn from them. What is one mistake you are very glad you made?

DATE Mo Tu We Th Fr Sa Su ___/___/___

I am grateful for...

Write about a nap you took recently and how you felt afterward.

STOP.

A good laugh and a long sleep are the two best cures for anything.

SMILE.

GO ON.

DATE Mo Tu We Th Fr Sa Su ___/___/___

I am grateful for...

Describe a dream that left you feeling happy upon waking.

THIS WEEK'S REFLECTION

Be a rainbow in someone's cloud.

Take the time to be kind. You can make all the difference in someone's day. You can simply smile, or show warmth to someone. You can give someone your time and truly listen to what they have to say. You can choose not to judge.

Kindness holds the power to transform both the giver and receiver. When we are kind, it improves our own emotional well-being, self-esteem and even physical health by lowering blood pressure and cortisol, a hormone closely linked to stress.

What could you do to make another person feel better?

Who or what inspires you to be a better person?

Think of 3 good things that happened this week:

DATE Mo Tu We Th Fr Sa Su ___/___/___

I am grateful for...

What's one way you helped someone else today?

DATE Mo Tu We Th Fr Sa Su ___/___/___

I am grateful for...

What's the quirkiest trait you appreciate about a friend or family member?

DATE Mo Tu We Th Fr Sa Su ___/___/___

I am grateful for...

Describe a moment of kindness you witnessed or received recently.

Mo Tu We Th Fr Sa Su

DATE ___/___/____

I am grateful for...

Remember something you accomplished, even though you doubted you would be able to.

STOP.

This is a reminder that you are strong, beautiful, and kind, and can handle anything this week throws at you.

REMEMBER.

GO ON.

Mo Tu We Th Fr Sa Su

DATE ___/___/____

I am grateful for...

Remember a moment when you didn't feel like doing something but did it anyway and felt amazing afterwards.

Mo Tu We Th Fr Sa Su

DATE ___/___/___

I am grateful for...

☼

Write down the last meme that made you chuckle.

☽

STOP.

Smile.

It is not illegal yet.

SMILE.

GO ON.

Mo Tu We Th Fr Sa Su

DATE ___/___/___

I am grateful for...

☼

Name a TV show or movie scene that never fails to make you laugh.

☽

To love others, you must first love and accept yourself.

When your cup is filled to the brim with love and acceptance of yourself, you are at peace with yourself. You are not in a constant need of approval, you don't project your issues onto others, you don't expect others to fill the void in your heart.
You can't pour from an empty cup. You need to love yourself first in order to be able to give love to others.

A Simple Practice for the Upcoming Week:

Start each day by writing a positive, affirming statement about yourself. Examples include "I accept myself just as I am" and "I am worthy of respect and kindness."

Think of 3 good things that happened this week:

Mo Tu We Th Fr Sa Su

DATE ___/___/___

I am grateful for...

Who in your life helps you to love yourself more?

Mo Tu We Th Fr Sa Su

DATE ___/___/___

I am grateful for...

Write down three ways you've grown or improved in the last year.

Mo Tu We Th Fr Sa Su

DATE ___/___/___

I am grateful for...

What is one thing your body allowed you to do today that you are thankful for?

Mo Tu We Th Fr Sa Su

DATE ___/___/___

I am grateful for...

When did you last enjoy some quiet time, and what did you do?

STOP.

Do something today that your future self will thank you for.

THINK.

GO ON.

Mo Tu We Th Fr Sa Su

DATE ___/___/___

I am grateful for...

What is one healthy habit you are thankful for sticking to? How has it improved your life?

DATE Mo Tu We Th Fr Sa Su ___/___/___

I am grateful for...

What part of your bedtime routine are you most thankful for?

STOP.

When it rains look for rainbows.
When it's dark look for stars.

THINK.

GO ON.

DATE Mo Tu We Th Fr Sa Su ___/___/___

I am grateful for...

What's an unexpected convenience or bit of good luck you had today?

THIS WEEK'S REFLECTION

Make time for yourself.

One habit that most of us fail to acknowledge is implementing some "me time" in our lives.

Do one small thing that you enjoy doing every single day. It is essential for your peace of mind. Whether you listen to your favorite music, read a book you love, watch a movie, write in your journal, or anything else for that matter, be sure to set aside some time for yourself in the day.

What self-care activities bring you feelings of joy and calm?

Dedicate some time today to one of them.

Think of 3 good things that happened this week:

Mo Tu We Th Fr Sa Su

DATE ___/___/___

I am grateful for...

What do you most enjoy about the time you spend by yourself?

Mo Tu We Th Fr Sa Su

DATE ___/___/___

I am grateful for...

What simple pleasure did you enjoy today that you are thankful for?

Mo Tu We Th Fr Sa Su

DATE ___/___/___

I am grateful for...

What's a color you saw today that you really liked?

Mo Tu We Th Fr Sa Su
DATE ___/___/___

I am grateful for...

Write about a humorous tradition or inside joke in your family or friend group.

STOP.

Today choose joy!

SMILE.

GO ON.

Mo Tu We Th Fr Sa Su
DATE ___/___/___

I am grateful for...

Think back to a joyful memory from your childhood.
What made it so special?

Mo Tu We Th Fr Sa Su

DATE ___/___/___

I am grateful for...

☼

Write about a moment when doing nothing felt absolutely right. What was that like?

☽

STOP.

Make today count. You will never get it back.

REMEMBER.

GO ON.

Mo Tu We Th Fr Sa Su

DATE ___/___/___

I am grateful for...

☼

Describe the texture of something you touched today. How did it feel against your skin?

☽

THIS WEEK'S REFLECTION

Your body hears everything your mind says.

Feeling down? Did you know that our bodies might respond to negative emotions with headaches, back pain, upset stomach, increased inflammation, unwanted weight gain or loss, to name a few?

That doesn't mean you need to deny your negative feelings. Acknowledge them but focus on something good. Direct your thoughts to something positive.

If you have negative thoughts don't slump over or bend your head. This will only validate them and make you feel worse.

Instead, write those thoughts down on a piece of paper, and then throw it away in the trash. This symbolic act will make you less affected by your negative thoughts.

Try it!

Think of 3 good things that happened this week:

____

____

____

Mo Tu We Th Fr Sa Su

DATE ___/___/___

I am grateful for...

Imagine a place that makes you feel peaceful and describe it.

Mo Tu We Th Fr Sa Su

DATE ___/___/___

I am grateful for...

Who are the people you can turn to when you're feeling down?

Mo Tu We Th Fr Sa Su

DATE ___/___/___

I am grateful for...

Write a compassionate message to yourself about your current struggles.

Mo Tu We Th Fr Sa Su

DATE ____/____/____

I am grateful for...

☼

How did you feel after the best sleep you've had recently?

☽

STOP.

When all else fails take a nap.

SMILE.

GO ON.

Mo Tu We Th Fr Sa Su

DATE ____/____/____

I am grateful for...

☼

Describe the pace of your day today. Was it fast, slow, uneven? How did you adapt?

☽

DATE Mo Tu We Th Fr Sa Su ___/___/___

I am grateful for...

Write about the last thing that made you pause and take a moment to reflect.

STOP.

Enjoy the little things,
for one day you may look back
and realize
they were the big things.

REMEMBER.
GO ON.

DATE Mo Tu We Th Fr Sa Su ___/___/___

I am grateful for...

Look around and name three objects you see that you hadn't noticed before.

THIS WEEK'S REFLECTION

If you can't be grateful, be quiet.

Complaining contrasts sharply with practicing gratitude, as it shifts focus to the negative aspects of life, reinforcing a pessimistic mindset. This habit of constantly complaining can dampen our mood, strain our relationships, and nurture a negative way of thinking.

This is in stark contrast to gratitude, which enhances our mood, strengthens our social connections, and promotes a positive outlook.

Essentially, gratitude enables us to feel happier and see the positive side of life, while complaining tends to bring us down. Therefore, embracing gratitude involves making an effort to complain less.

What is one negative thought you had recently?
How can you reframe it into something positive or constructive?

Think of 3 good things that happened this week:

Mo Tu We Th Fr Sa Su

DATE ___/___/___

I am grateful for...

List self-care activities that make you feel better when you're down.

Mo Tu We Th Fr Sa Su

DATE ___/___/___

I am grateful for...

Recall one good thing that came out of a situation that initially seemed negative?

Mo Tu We Th Fr Sa Su

DATE ___/___/___

I am grateful for...

When was the last time you admired a beautiful view?

Mo Tu We Th Fr Sa Su

DATE ___/___/___

I am grateful for...

Recall a moment from today that made you smile.

STOP.

Every new day is another chance to change your life.

REMEMBER.

GO ON.

Mo Tu We Th Fr Sa Su

DATE ___/___/___

I am grateful for...

List three desires you have that you intend to honor and pursue, and why they are important to you.

DATE Mo Tu We Th Fr Sa Su ___/___/___

I am grateful for...

What was the most peaceful moment of your day and how did it make you feel?

STOP.

When you shift your focus from your defeats to your victories, you'll see that life ain't that bad. You're winning.

THINK.

GO ON.

DATE Mo Tu We Th Fr Sa Su ___/___/___

I am grateful for...

Acknowledge something difficult about your day that you accepted without self-criticism.

THIS WEEK'S REFLECTION

*You cannot travel back in time
to fix your mistakes,
but you can learn from them
and forgive yourself for not knowing better.*

At some point you just have to let go of what you thought should or should not happen and live in what is happening.

Think of a negative event in your past.
How can you use it as an opportunity to grow?

Think of 3 good things that happened this week:

DATE Mo Tu We Th Fr Sa Su ___/___/___

I am grateful for...

Reflect on a time you felt peace with who you are in the present moment.

DATE Mo Tu We Th Fr Sa Su ___/___/___

I am grateful for...

Recall a moment where you felt true to yourself, despite external pressures.

DATE Mo Tu We Th Fr Sa Su ___/___/___

I am grateful for...

What, if anything, went wrong today and how can you do better tomorrow?

Mo Tu We Th Fr Sa Su

DATE ___/___/___

I am grateful for...

What's a favorite item of clothing that you wore?

STOP.

How to be happy (101):
Decide every morning
that you are in a good mood.

SMILE.
GO ON.

Mo Tu We Th Fr Sa Su

DATE ___/___/___

I am grateful for...

What did you enjoy the most about today and why?

DATE Mo Tu We Th Fr Sa Su ___/___/___

I am grateful for...

What part of your health are you most grateful for today?

STOP.

Acknowledging the good that you already have in your life is the foundation for all abundance.

THINK.

GO ON.

DATE Mo Tu We Th Fr Sa Su ___/___/___

I am grateful for...

Who in your life are you most grateful for today, and why?

THIS WEEK'S REFLECTION

You are only human.

Forgive yourself for what you have done and what you think you should have done or not.

One bad deed does not make a good person bad. Just like one good act does not redeem the previous bad actions. At every moment you have had your reasons for the actions and decisions you have taken.

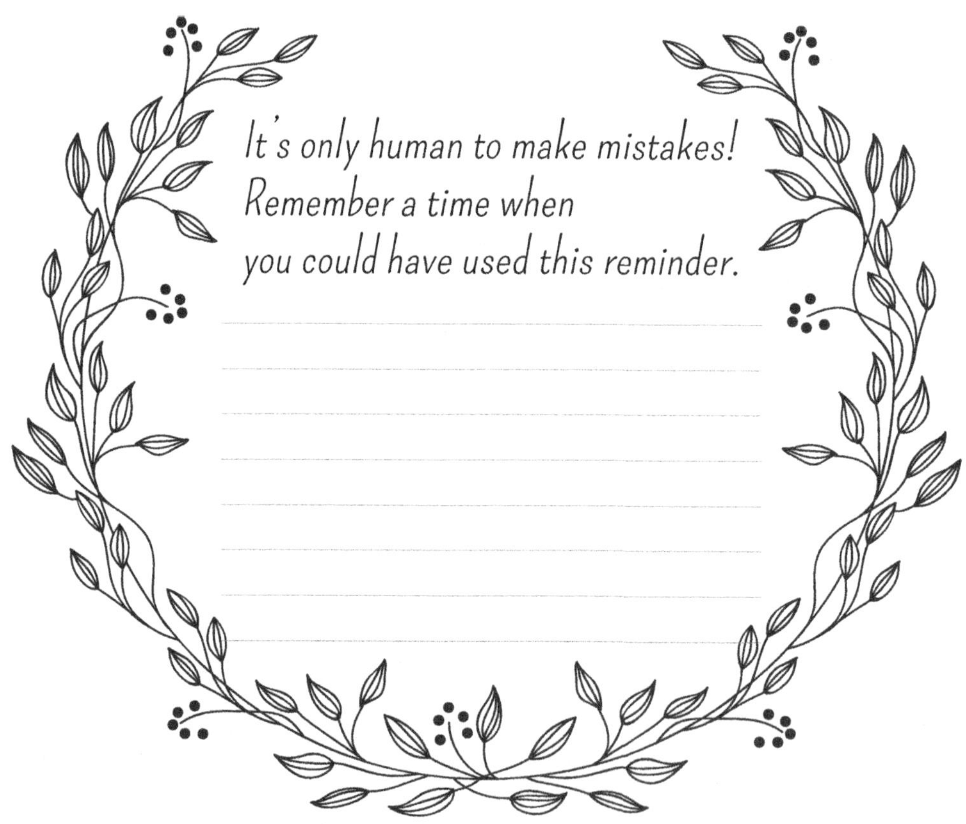

It's only human to make mistakes! Remember a time when you could have used this reminder.

Think of 3 good things that happened this week:

Mo Tu We Th Fr Sa Su

DATE ___/___/___

I am grateful for...

Name one thing you're looking forward to this week.

Mo Tu We Th Fr Sa Su

DATE ___/___/___

I am grateful for...

What line from a book or article resonated with you today and why?

Mo Tu We Th Fr Sa Su

DATE ___/___/___

I am grateful for...

Share a "good news" story that brought a smile to your face.

Mo Tu We Th Fr Sa Su

DATE ___/___/___

I am grateful for...

What small thing did you find beautiful today and why?

STOP.

Laugh, live, love!
No one on their deathbed has ever said,
"I wish I worked more".

REMEMBER.

GO ON.

Mo Tu We Th Fr Sa Su

DATE ___/___/___

I am grateful for...

What moment today did you fully engage in, without distraction?

Mo Tu We Th Fr Sa Su

DATE ___/___/___

I am grateful for...

Share the best dad joke you've heard recently.

STOP.

If you are in a bad mood
go for a walk.
If you are still in a bad mood
go for another walk.

SMILE.
GO ON.

Mo Tu We Th Fr Sa Su

DATE ___/___/___

I am grateful for...

When today did you feel most at peace, and what were you doing?

THIS WEEK'S REFLECTION

The people around you matter.

You are who you hang out with, so choose your friends wisely and carefully. Surround yourself with people who are positive, kind, supportive and don't make you question your worth. Spend time with those who make you feel happy and fulfilled. This will increase your own positivity and happiness levels.

Who are the people you spend the most time with?

Who is the most positive person you know?
How do you feel when you are around him or her?

Think of 3 good things that happened this week:

Mo Tu We Th Fr Sa Su

DATE ___/___/___

I am grateful for...

What do you want to take from today into tomorrow?

Mo Tu We Th Fr Sa Su

DATE ___/___/___

I am grateful for...

Name one person whose company you enjoyed today?

Mo Tu We Th Fr Sa Su

DATE ___/___/___

I am grateful for...

What's your favorite smell or scent?

Mo Tu We Th Fr Sa Su

DATE ___/___/___

I am grateful for...

What made you smile today? It could be as simple as a sunny day, a good cup of coffee, or a funny text from a friend.

STOP.

Happiness can be...
not having to set the alarm for the next day.

SMILE.

GO ON.

Mo Tu We Th Fr Sa Su

DATE ___/___/___

I am grateful for...

If you cannot meet in person, pick up the phone and connect with a good friend for a quick dose of happiness. Who will you call?

DATE Mo Tu We Th Fr Sa Su ___/___/___

I am grateful for...

Recall a small victory or accomplishment from this week.

STOP.

Don't count the days.
Make the days count.

THINK.
GO ON.

DATE Mo Tu We Th Fr Sa Su ___/___/___

I am grateful for...

At what moment today did you pause and what did you notice during that pause?

THIS WEEK'S REFLECTION

In solitude the mind gains strength and learns to lean upon itself.

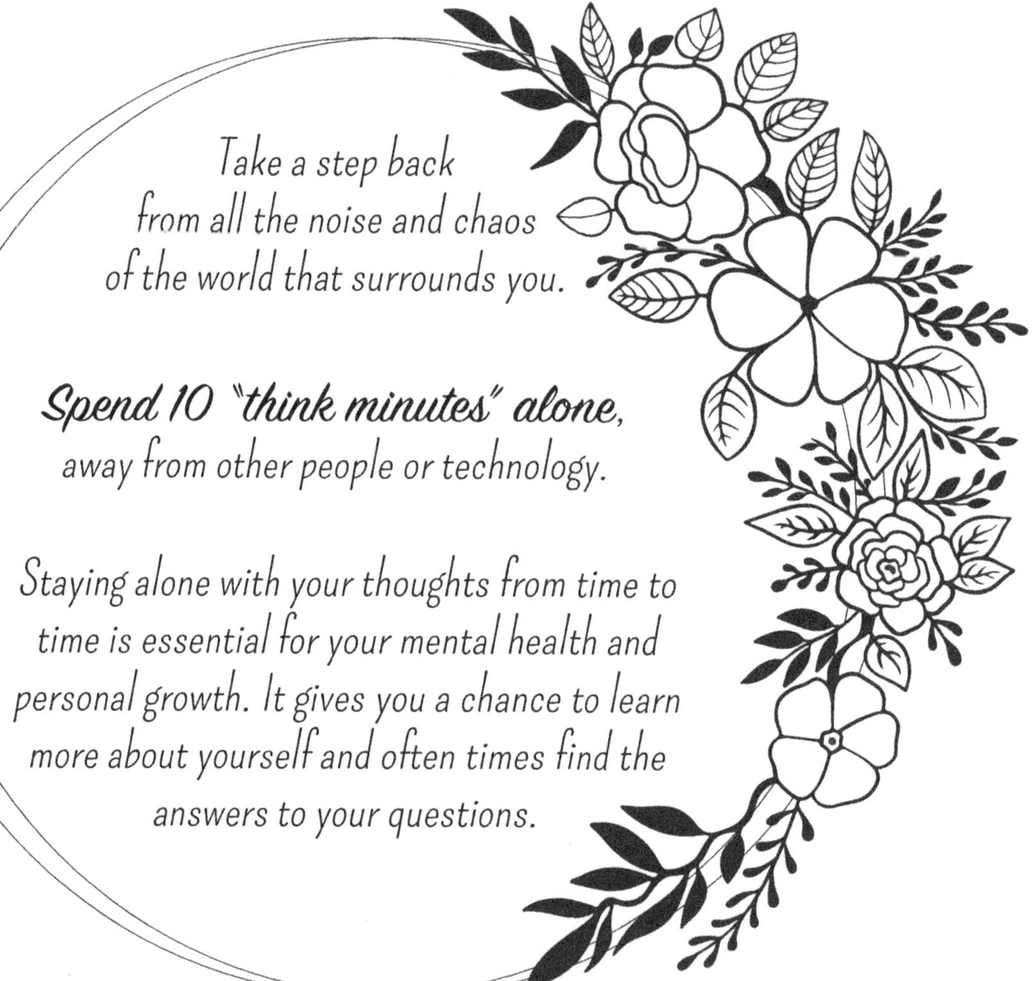

Take a step back
from all the noise and chaos
of the world that surrounds you.

Spend 10 "think minutes" alone,
away from other people or technology.

Staying alone with your thoughts from time to time is essential for your mental health and personal growth. It gives you a chance to learn more about yourself and often times find the answers to your questions.

Think of 3 good things that happened this week:

DATE Mo Tu We Th Fr Sa Su ___/___/___

I am grateful for...

What are three mini-goals that you can smash this week?

DATE Mo Tu We Th Fr Sa Su ___/___/___

I am grateful for...

Recall a memory associated with a beloved song and why it's special to you.

DATE Mo Tu We Th Fr Sa Su ___/___/___

I am grateful for...

What was the last thing that made you laugh out loud?

Mo Tu We Th Fr Sa Su

DATE ___/___/___

I am grateful for...

Describe your current environment in detail. What do you notice that you usually overlook?

STOP.

Yesterday is history.
Tomorrow is a mystery.
Today is a gift.
That is why it is called the present.

SMILE.
GO ON.

Mo Tu We Th Fr Sa Su

DATE ___/___/___

I am grateful for...

What sounds can you hear right now? List them and describe their qualities (loud, soft, rhythmic, etc.).

DATE Mo Tu We Th Fr Sa Su ___/___/___

I am grateful for...

Think about the people you love. How do you add happiness to their life?

STOP.

You can give without loving,
but you cannot love without giving.

REMEMBER.
GO ON.

DATE Mo Tu We Th Fr Sa Su ___/___/___

I am grateful for...

Think of a time when someone showed you such generosity that you thought, "Wow, I can't believe they did that for me."

THIS WEEK'S REFLECTION

Plan a date with yourself.

Taking yourself on a date can be empowering, uplifting, and do miracles for your mind and acceptance. This is one of the most effective and fun ways to practice self-love and you deserve it!

Plan your date.

» Choose an activity that you think you will truly enjoy. You may go out for dinner and a movie, book a spa treatment, take yourself on a picnic, or go for a walk.

» Put your solo date on your calendar and make sure to show up. Don't ghost yourself!

» Get dressed up and do whatever you need to do to feel good about yourself.

» Treat it like you would treat any date with another person. Make it special!

Think of 3 good things that happened this week:

______

______

______

DATE Mo Tu We Th Fr Sa Su ___/___/___

I am grateful for...

What is bringing you joy at this very moment?

DATE Mo Tu We Th Fr Sa Su ___/___/___

I am grateful for...

What is one thing you did today to relax and unwind?

DATE Mo Tu We Th Fr Sa Su ___/___/___

I am grateful for...

What was the strongest emotion you felt today?

Mo Tu We Th Fr Sa Su

DATE ___/___/___

I am grateful for...

Imagine your perfect day and write about what it would look like.

STOP.

Be patient with yourself.
Nothing in nature blooms all year.

THINK.

GO ON.

Mo Tu We Th Fr Sa Su

DATE ___/___/___

I am grateful for...

Think of something that has bothered you lately. Do you think you will still care about it in a month? Or in a year?

DATE Mo Tu We Th Fr Sa Su ___/___/___

I am grateful for...

Consider a recent challenge. What positive lessons or strengths did you gain from it?

STOP.

Instead of being ashamed of what you've been through, be proud of what you have overcome!

THINK.

GO ON.

DATE Mo Tu We Th Fr Sa Su ___/___/___

I am grateful for...

Think of a time you were proud of yourself.
What happened and how did you feel?

THIS WEEK'S REFLECTION

Research shows that spending time in nature, or enjoying pockets of green in urban settings, has been found to reduce stress and negative emotions, and help with mental health problems such as anxiety and depression.

Get outside for some green time!

Or create your own green space by planting some flowers or your own vegetables, which can have a similar effect.

If you had a garden that could grow anything, what would you grow?

Think of 3 good things that happened this week:

DATE Mo Tu We Th Fr Sa Su ___/___/___

I am grateful for...

When was the last time you enjoyed being out in nature?

DATE Mo Tu We Th Fr Sa Su ___/___/___

I am grateful for...

Do you have a favorite flower? What is it?

DATE Mo Tu We Th Fr Sa Su ___/___/___

I am grateful for...

If you could travel anywhere in the world for any length of time, where would it be?

DATE Mo Tu We Th Fr Sa Su ___/___/___

I am grateful for...

What moments from today do you want to remember?

STOP.

It takes sunshine and rain to make a rainbow.

REMEMBER.
GO ON.

DATE Mo Tu We Th Fr Sa Su ___/___/___

I am grateful for...

Do a quick mental scan of your body from head to toe. What sensations or feelings do you notice?

DATE Mo Tu We Th Fr Sa Su ___/___/___

I am grateful for...

What skills do you want to learn or improve?

STOP.

The man who moves a mountain begins by carrying away small stones.

REMEMBER.

GO ON.

DATE Mo Tu We Th Fr Sa Su ___/___/___

I am grateful for...

Reflect on a time when you remained strong during a difficult period. How did you manage to keep going?

THIS WEEK'S REFLECTION

It's not what you are that holds you back, it's what you think you are not.

We often hold back from doing things because we think "I can't do that", or "That's not for me", or above all "I am not [smart/pretty/consistent/motivated/adventurous/etc.] enough to do it". We are held back by the very limits we set for ourselves.

Trust yourself—you know and can more than you think you do.

Recall a time when you succeeded at something you initially doubted you could do. Write about what this experience taught you.

Think of 3 good things that happened this week:

DATE Mo Tu We Th Fr Sa Su ___/___/___

I am grateful for...

Think of a stereotype that applies to you. How have you proven it wrong in your life?

DATE Mo Tu We Th Fr Sa Su ___/___/___

I am grateful for...

What personal values are you proud of?

DATE Mo Tu We Th Fr Sa Su ___/___/___

I am grateful for...

What's a lesson you learned from a recent challenge that you now appreciate?

Mo Tu We Th Fr Sa Su

DATE ___/___/___ *I am grateful for...*

Write down a positive affirmation about yourself. Why do you believe this affirmation to be true?

STOP.

The only thing standing between you and your goal is the BS story you keep telling yourself as to why you can't achieve it.

REMEMBER.

GO ON.

Mo Tu We Th Fr Sa Su

DATE ___/___/___ *I am grateful for...*

Pause to identify how you are feeling right now. Can you observe your emotions without judgment?

Mo Tu We Th Fr Sa Su

DATE ___/___/___

I am grateful for...

Describe a piece of clothing or an accessory you used today that you're thankful for.

STOP.

Life gets so much better when you cut the negative BS out. The only BS allowed should be Bags and Shoes.

SMILE.

GO ON.

Mo Tu We Th Fr Sa Su

DATE ___/___/___

I am grateful for...

Step outside and take a deep breath. What does the air feel like? What scents do you detect?

THIS WEEK'S REFLECTION

Be kind to your mind.

In a world that constantly pushes us towards productivity and perfection, it's really important to be kind to ourselves, especially our thoughts and feelings. This means noticing when things are hard and giving ourselves a chance to rest or get help, instead of just keeping going until we're too tired.

Being kind to our own minds helps us become stronger, think more positively about ourselves, and feel more at peace. Doing this can make us feel happier, have better relationships with others, and enjoy life more.

Whenever you notice self-criticism or negative thoughts about yourself,

take a brief "self-compassion break."

This involves pausing for a few moments, placing your hand on your heart, and offering yourself kind words, just as you would to a friend in need. Acknowledge your feelings, remind yourself that imperfection is part of the shared human experience, and offer yourself the understanding and kindness you would extend to others.

Think of 3 good things that happened this week:

DATE Mo Tu We Th Fr Sa Su ___/___/___

I am grateful for...

☼

What emotion did you feel today that you are thankful for, even if it was challenging?

☽

DATE Mo Tu We Th Fr Sa Su ___/___/___

I am grateful for...

☼

Finish this sentence: "My life would be incomplete without ..."

☽

DATE Mo Tu We Th Fr Sa Su ___/___/___

I am grateful for...

☼

What is one mistake you made today, and did you show kindness to yourself afterward?

☽

DATE Mo Tu We Th Fr Sa Su ___/___/___

I am grateful for...

List three things you're looking forward to doing tomorrow.

STOP.

Tomorrow (noun) – a mystical land where 99% of all human productivity, motivation and achievement is stored.

SMILE.
GO ON.

DATE Mo Tu We Th Fr Sa Su ___/___/___

I am grateful for...

When was the last time you tried something new? Review your bucket list or create one, and think about one activity you would love to cross off first!

DATE Mo Tu We Th Fr Sa Su ___/___/___

I am grateful for...

What is one habit you want to start?

STOP.

Happiness is the highest form of health.

THINK.
GO ON.

DATE Mo Tu We Th Fr Sa Su ___/___/___

I am grateful for...

Express gratitude for access to healthcare or a particular healthcare professional who has helped you.

THIS WEEK'S REFLECTION

You are good enough.

Get it through your head that it doesn't matter how you look, how many wrinkles you have, how much you are overweight, how many dimples there are on your thighs. It doesn't matter that you are overly sensitive, socially awkward, irrational at times, terrible at math, not environment friendly enough, or that you make mistakes.
YOU ARE STILL GOOD ENOUGH.

You are imperfect. But you are worthy of love and belonging.

Fill in the blanks:

It doesn't matter that ... ____________________ *I AM STILL ENOUGH!*

It doesn't matter that ... ____________________ *I AM STILL ENOUGH!*

It doesn't matter that ... ____________________ *I AM STILL ENOUGH!*

It doesn't matter that ... ____________________ *I AM STILL ENOUGH!*

It doesn't matter that ... ____________________ *I AM STILL ENOUGH!*

Think of 3 good things that happened this week:

____

____

____

DATE Mo Tu We Th Fr Sa Su ___/___/___

I am grateful for...

Who inspires you to believe in yourself?

DATE Mo Tu We Th Fr Sa Su ___/___/___

I am grateful for...

What's an imperfection you have that you're thankful for because it makes you unique?

DATE Mo Tu We Th Fr Sa Su ___/___/___

I am grateful for...

What is one thing you find beautiful about your body today?

Mo Tu We Th Fr Sa Su

DATE ___/___/___

I am grateful for...

Write down a compliment to yourself for something you did today.

STOP.

This page breezes in to tell you that:

You are doing great.
Take care of yourself in a healthy way.
Rest if needed. Chasing after your goals is admirable but know that you are enough always, regardless of the results.

REMEMBER.

GO ON.

Mo Tu We Th Fr Sa Su

DATE ___/___/___

I am grateful for...

What three things would you most like others (loved ones, potential friends and partners, professional acquaintances, etc.) to know about you?

Mo Tu We Th Fr Sa Su

DATE ___/___/___

I am grateful for...

Imagine your perfect vacation and write about what it would look like.

STOP.

Happiness cannot be traveled to, owned, earned, worn or consumed. Happiness is the spiritual experience of living every minute with love, grace, and gratitude.

REMEMBER.

GO ON.

Mo Tu We Th Fr Sa Su

DATE ___/___/___

I am grateful for...

Dedicate a few minutes today to imagine your happiest self. Write about how you will feel, what you will have, what you will be grateful for.

Hey gorgeous!

We are Happiness Creators.

We believe that everyone deserves to be happy, healthy, and loved. We create all our books and journals passionately with one goal in mind: to improve and add joy to people's lives. Hopefully this journal will accomplish just that for you.

HELP US MAKE OUR JOURNAL BETTER.

We're committed to improving our journals and we'd love your help! Let us know which page you enjoyed the most. Was there anything that didn't quite meet your expectations? Share your thoughts on what changes or additions you'd like to see.
Your feedback, whether it's suggestions, recommendations, or critiques, is invaluable to us. We promise to consider each piece of feedback carefully and strive to incorporate it into our future editions.

We'd love to hear from you, even if it is just to say hi. And there is nothing more gratifying to us and putting more meaning to our work than hearing that our books have helped you.

Contact us at: **hello@happinesscreators.com**

And please, ***leave a review***, it really helps us!

Take care and have a beautiful day,

Happiness Creators